W9-BJC-239

TREATING THE AFRICAN AMERICAN MALE SUBSTANCE ABUSER

BY

MARK SANDERS, LCSW, CADC

I hope all is well
with you. May your
life be filled with
success, peace,
happiness and joy.

Mark

Copyright © 1993
Winds of Change Publishing Company
230 N. Michigan, Suite 2900, Chicago, IL 60601
(312) 549-7914

Cover designed by Robert Reese

All rights in this book are reserved. No part of the text
may be produced in any form without written permission
of the publisher, except brief quotations used in connection with review in journals, magazines or newspapers.

ISBN 0-9637910-0-1
Printed in the United States of America

ACKNOWLEDGEMENTS

I would like to thank my wife, Tanya Sanders who helped give me the inspiration to write this book by writing with me every Sunday in our two-person book writing club.

Special thanks to my brother, William, who continuously encouraged me to finish this work. He led by example, as a result of completing a screenplay of his own.

Finally, great thanks to my mother, who always encouraged me to have independent thought.

SPECIAL THANKS

To my best friend, Desi, for being there throughout my life.

To my step father, Sidney, for being a good role model.

To Robert Reese, who designed the book cover.

To Mirek from Compu-All computer service for typesetting the manuscript.

To Susan Rentle, my first social work Professor at MacMurray College, who taught me how to help others.

TABLE OF CONTENTS

CHAPTER   TITLE   PAGE

INTRODUCTION

I have had the opportunity to travel throughout Chicago and the surrounding suburbs to assess the substance abuse treatment needs of clients receiving hospital treatment on inpatient, for-profit substance abuse units. I was always astounded by the number of African American Males receiving treatment in these hospital facilities. Seventy-five percent of the patients in one facility, located in a predominantly white community were African American Males. A phone survey of treatment providers located in suburban areas, with less than a 1% African American residency, indicated that often 10% to 40% of the patients were African American Males. During my 2-1/2 years of clinical assessments for a major automobile industry, over 85% of the clients requesting chemical dependence treatment were African American males.

African American Males are also disproportionately represented as clients in central city, not-for-profit substance abuse treatment facilities and halfway houses. In addition, our nation's jails are filled with African American male substance abusers who have committed crimes to support drug habits.

Having had the opportunity to work with African American male patients in settings that were predominantly staffed by White workers and in turn settings that were predominantly staffed by African American employees, I have seen first-hand that most individuals are perplexed as to how to provide culturally-sensitive treatment to this special population.

Staff members typically have questions when treating African American male patients such as "How do I deal with their anger? Are they an anti-social personality? Do I speak slang to them or standard English? Should I confront them? Do I relate to them as a "brother" or as a client? How do I talk to them about sexual issues in treatment? Should I feel guilty because they are complaining about injustices done to them by Whites, because I am a White counselor? How Do I get them to see that they are suffering from a disease and need to admit powerlessness, when all their lives they have been told that they have to be powerful and strong? Is it okay to touch them? What do I do if they cry?" The answers to these questions and many more will be addressed in this book.

The main reason I have written this book is because there are so many unanswered questions about the way to treat African American male patients, that I believe they are at much greater risk for relapse than the general population. The more we learn about providing culturally-sensitive treatment for the African American male substance abuser, the greater their chances of sobriety will be.

CHAPTER I

A HISTORICAL PERSPECTIVE OF SUBSTANCE ABUSE AND THE AFRICAN AMERICAN MALE

Currently, it is estimated that one out of every ten dollars spent in the African American community is spent on alcohol. It is also estimated that over half of the African American males incarcerated in the criminal justice system for crimes such as murder, rape and robbery were under the influence of alcohol while committing these crimes.

Today, eight of the leading causes of death for African-American males in their mid-twenties include:

Homicide
Motor Vehicle Accidents
Cirrhosis
Suicide
Heart Attacks
Stroke
Pneumonia
Diabetes

One does not have to be an expert on chemical dependence to know that many of these causes of death could be alcohol and/or drug-related. Cirrhosis, heart attacks, strokes, pneumonia and diabetes can be symptoms of, or exacerbated by, chemical dependence. We all know that there is an increased risk of homicide, car accidents and suicide when substance abuse is involved. In short, I believe that the leading cause of death for young adult African American males is chemical dependence. Of course, the obvious question is why?

Historically, African-American male slaves were not allowed to drink alcohol with their slave masters. Most slave states had laws that prohibited slaves from drinking in public. This precaution was in place because of fear of angry outbursts and riots on the part of slaves.

For the most part, African American men were not allowed to drink publicly until the Civil War. During this time, Whites were unable to control the intake of alcohol on the part of the slaves because they were busy fighting the war.

With reconstruction and the end of slavery, came the drinking of more alcohol on the part of the African-American male. Their response was similar to the response of a teenager after the parent has constantly told them that participating in a certain behavior is not okay. The teen will often rebel and engage in the behavior anyway. Thus, African Americans , after being restricted from drinking alcohol for so long, rebelled and began to drink with an incredible zeal.

Following the end of slavery, African Americans had to find ways of making a living. It would have been natural for

African American males to feel intense pressure because it was believed that the financial responsibility for supporting the family was a male responsibility. For the next 200 years, a combination of no education, miseducation, discrimination, lack of opportunity and self-pity has caused many African-American men to give up on the "American Dream" and to medicate and numb themselves with alcohol and other drugs from the reality of not achieving the American dream.

Wars, especially the Vietnam War, have also played a major role in the chemical dependence crisis that now confronts African American males. Many young African American males were drafted. Others, eager to do good for their country, enlisted into the Armed Forces. This unwinnable pressure-packed war led to much chemical abuse on the part of the soldier while in combat, in an attempt to numb themselves from the reality of their situation. This substance abuse often continued when they returned to the United States. The Vietnam war allowed African Americans to be introduced, on a larger scale than ever before, to other drugs besides alcohol (i.e., heroin, hashish, marijuana, opium, etc). The counter-cultural "revolution" of the 1960's also introduced African Americans to other kinds of drugs, including LSD and other hallucinogens.

In the 1970's and 1980's African Americans began to use cocaine. Many have theorized that cocaine was the drug of the 70's and 80's because our society turned into the "me" generation. Cocaine offered the ultimate pleasure for an individual. I believe the drug was attractive to African American men for several reasons:

1) The myth that the drug was not very addictive;
2) A status symbol for some middle class African American males;
3) A self destructive solution to self Hate (Chapter 2);
4) The sexual myth affiliated with the drug (Chapter 7);
5) The stimulating effect of the drug makes them feel more grandiose, powerful and in control (very impor tant in a society where individuals feel that they have no control);
6) The income generated from the drug gave many African American males another avenue for becom ing entrepreneurs; selling drugs became another source of income (Chapter 8).

Today, the onset of addiction for African American males

appears to be getting younger and younger as crack cocaine has invaded central cities. Drug selling has increased which contributes to the public school drop out rate as selling drugs offers a quicker rate of success than academic pursuits.

CHAPTER II

SELF-HATE AS A CONTRIBUTING FACTOR

The inspiration for this chapter was an Oprah Winfrey show which focused on racism against Native-Americans. On this thought-provoking program, the Native-American panel of experts talked about how the hundreds of years of negative images presented by the American media contributed to Native-American low self-concept. One expert on the show pointed out that the suicide rate for Native-American children is twice the rate of the general population and that low self-esteem is a major contributing factor.

400 years of the American experience has also led to extremely low self-esteem and self-hatred for many African-Americans. During slavery, African Americans were told by Whites that they were a cursed people, destined to be slaves because they were descendants of HAM. The Old Testament (Genesis, Chapter 9) describes a scene in which Noah got drunk and took off all his clothes. His youngest son, Ham, saw his father naked and told his two brothers, Shem and Japneth. They in turn took a blanket and covered Noah's nakedness. When Noah awoke from his intoxication, he became angry with Ham and made him a slave. African American slaves were thus taught by their slave masters that they were the descendants of Ham during church services. What is the psychological impact of being told that you are a slave because of a religious mandate? If a group of people internalize even a portion of this belief, they can't help but feel a degree of inferiority. This ideology existed for a number of generations. It has been passed down from generation to generation through oral tradition. Even

today, in 1993, many African Americans are aware of the effort to link them with Ham.

I recently presented a seminar on African-Americans and substance abuse to a racially-mixed audience and I asked the question, "How many of you are aware that African American slaves were told that they were destined to be slaves because they were descendants of Ham?" None of the White participants were aware of this, while all of the African Americans were familiar with these teachings.

Abandonment has also played a major role in the self-hatred of African-Americans. John Bradshaw, in a film entitled "Shame and Addiction", points out that abandonment leads to toxic shame. A toxically, shame-based person feels worthless and useless. They believe that they are a mistake and that they should not have been born. Bradshaw points out that since young children idealize their parents, when they are abandoned they blame themselves and begin to believe it happened because they are bad children. This is often the beginning of self-contempt and ultimately self-hate.

The history of African-Americans in America is a history of continuous abandonment. The act of being taken from Africa against their wills and forced into slavery was a major form of abandonment. These people were robbed of their right to be human. Early slave families were often separated, for anyone in the family could be sold at any time, which created the possibility of never seeing each other again. This situation was the ultimate abandonment.

America's unequal treatment of African-Americans following the end of slavery has constituted yet another form of abandonment. Especially when one considers how hard African Americans worked to help build America.

In the film "Shame and Addiction", Bradshaw points out that abandonment in families is multi-generational. Those who have been abandoned marry people who will abandon them and this cycle continues generation after generation after generation. Is there a multi-generational transmission of abandonment operating in the African-American community today? Are African Americans today still affected by the early abandonment experience of their ancestors in slavery?

One of the things I have learned in my work as a psychotherapist is that parents who abandon their children were usually abandoned by their parents when they where children. They may never have had the opportunity to talk about the abandonment they experienced as a child and are therefore unconsciously doing the same thing to their children. Effective intervention and treatment involves helping such a parent get in touch with their own childhood abandonment issues, so that they will understand why they abandon their own children. This is a very painful process and most people do not want to talk about it. This is the African-American story! There has been so much abandonment in the African-American community, so many losses since slavery, that it is often too painful to talk about. When it can't be talked about, it will be repeated.

I do believe there is a multigenerational transmission process of abandonment operating in the African-American community and that the process has become internalized, for today, a great deal of abandonment occurs within the race. Since African Americans migrated from the south to the north, there has been a continuous breakdown of extended family bonds, and a decrease in the number of adults emotionally available for the children. The African concept of "it takes a village to raise a child" continues to erode each decade. The increase in teenage pregnancy in the African American community and therefore parents being too young emotionally themselves to help meet the child's emotional needs is another form of abandonment.

African American fathers leaving the family is yet another form of abandonment. The feeling of being abandoned is compounded if it is not talked about. In many African-American families, the fathers leave home and this is never discussed. It is amazing how many children who are seen in therapy do not know why their father left home. As mentioned earlier, children blame themselves for all forms of abandonment. Abandonment is further compounded if it is not talked about, because the child unconsciously believes they must have done something terrible to make their parent leave. In fact, the child believes that whatever they did was so bad that it cannot be talked about. This thought process produces self-contempt and self-hatred.

The Importance Of Fathers

Many people say basketball is a "Black man's" game. I believe that there is an additional variable that must be examined. It is my opinion that basketball, at the highest level, is played by men who generally had very strong male and female influences while growing up.

The 1992 U.S. Olympic men's basketball team, nick-named "The Dream Team", is considered by many to be the greatest basketball team ever assembled. Most of the players were raised by both parents. Significantly, Magic Johnson, Larry Bird and Michael Jordan, the three most influential players in modern basketball, were all raised by both parents.

On a recent Phil Donahue show, John Bradshaw discussed a study that found that children who lived with fathers had a greater ability to delay gratification than children from homes with absent fathers. Bradshaw stated that he believes the reason for this finding is that "fathers represent security", and when fathers are present, kids do not feel pressured into having to make quick decisions.

If there were less abandonment by fathers in the African American community, would the teenage pregnancy rate decrease? Would African American youth be better able to delay gratification or perhaps feel less of a need to have a baby to fill the void? Does both emotional and physical abandonment contribute to the substance abuse problems of African-American males? This would make a great research study, especially when you consider that addiction is partially about looking for instant gratification.

Many young African American fathers leave their families because they feel overwhelmed. This feeling is often attributed to believing that they cannot meet all the responsibilities of being the head of a household as defined by America. Perhaps we would see a decrease in abandonment by fathers if the concept of manhood were redefined. Jawanza Kunjufu, in the book "Countering The Conspiracy To Destroy Black Boys, Volume II" (1986), states "I have observed different responses from unemployed fathers. Some fathers cry in their misery and make the matters worse with abuse, neglect and crime. While other fathers under the same circumstances will sell papers or peanuts, or provide landscaping or garbage removal service. Should African American men and women accept these narrow gender roles, or understand that even while unemployed, they can help their children with homework, teach them the beauty of being unashamedly African American , unapologetically Christian and assist their wives with housework."

A social work colleague of mine suggested that instead of studying why African American teenage fathers leave, we should do research studies about those who stay. Once we understand those dynamics that increase the probability that fathers will stay, social programs could reflect those findings.

In closing this section, it must be stated that African American fathers do not have a monopoly on abandonment. It is getting easier for fathers to leave families across cultures. I presented this data to point out how important African American fathers are. It should also be pointed out that many single parents do an outstanding job of raising children.

Others Factors Contributing To African-American Self-Hate.

Skin Color

During slavery, the rape of Black female slaves by white male slave masters produced children of various skin complexions. The lighter-skinned slaves were allowed to work inside the slave master's dwelling, while the darker-skinned slaves continued to pick cotton in the fields. This is how the terms "house nigger" and "field nigger" emerged. The lighter-skinned African Americans were treated better by Whites. What emerged was a progressive self-hate of dark skin among African-Americans.

When I was growing up in Chicago, there was a commonly held belief in the African American community, that lighter-skinned African Americans moved to the far south side of Chicago to separate themselves from the darker-skinned African Americans . Today, a number of my African-American psychotherapy clients complain of a belief that their parents gave preferential treatment to their lighter-skinned siblings. One of my lighter-skinned African American clients expressed the belief that her light skin has been a big advantage to her within her family, in dating and in the work world. In the book "Autobiography Of Malcolm X" by Alex Haley, Malcolm described his father as being very physically abusive. He expressed the opinion that his father was less physically abusive towards him because Malcolm was lighter-skinned than his other siblings.

Hair Texture

Inter-racial babies often have a thinner, less curly-at-the-roots hair texture than other African Americans . Progressively throughout the years, this hair texture (which is closer to the hair texture of many Whites) has been seen within the African-American race as being better than the curly African hair texture. When I was growing up, many African Americans would say that a person had "good hair" if the texture was close to that of Whites and that they had "bad hair" if they had the curly African hair texture. What is the psychological impact of this on one's self-concept? One result has been the hatred expressed toward African hair. This feeling has led to African-Americans doing all kinds of things through out the ages to make their hair straighter.

What's In A Name?

Throughout American history, there have been numerous terms used to describe African-Americans. some of the more common terms include:; "Negroes", "Niggers",

"Coons", "Colored people", "Blacks" and "African-Americans". The term "Blacks" has been used most often. Webster's dictionary defines black as "dirty, evil, wicked, sad and dismal". What is the psychological impact of being identified with a term that has such negative connotations? In fact, many words associated with the term black are also negative: "black-ball", "black-list", "black magic", "blackmail", "black mark", "black market", etc.

In addition, terms like 'negro', 'colored' and 'Black' do not suggest any cultural roots. If a person is Mexican-American, we know by the name that they have Mexican and American roots. Something to be proud of. The same is true for Japanese-Americans, Italian-Americans, etc., but, if you are "Black " or "Negro", what do you belong to?

I believe that the most dignified term to describe Blacks in America is "African-Americans". This term is the most accurate, because it identifies the group as having African and American roots. In addition, this term does the most for this groups self-concept because it fulfills the need that all human beings have; that is, the need to belong.

The Media

It is no secret that, historically, the American media has often portrayed African Americans in a negative light. In the 1940's, 50's and 60's, they were portrayed as lazy, non-intelligent "shufflers". More recently, they have been portrayed as gang-bangers, pimps, prostitutes, thieves, drug addicts, drug dealers, etc. This psychologically contributes to the way people see themselves. The emergence of the African-American screen writers such as John Singleton and Spike Lee, could be instrumental in increasing the range of African American images in the movies.

News programs often show minority males being arrested. This can psychologically contribute to one believing that jail is their destiny. Cable and public television programs present documentaries on Africa. Most of these documentaries show Africans starving, malnutritious, dying and surrounded by flies. Do these images make African-

American children feel proud of their African roots? Or, does it contribute to the self-hate of their African origins? Would their view of their heritage be different if they were shown self-supporting African societies, kings and queens, Great African technology, universities, African professionals, infrastructures that could compete with those in American and African contributions to civilizations?

History

I was having a discussion with a social worker who identifies herself as a feminist. She informed me that male superiority is promoted in U.S. history courses simply by spending more time focusing on male historical accomplishments than female accomplishments.

How much time is spent in U.S. History courses discussing African-American contributions? How much does this contribute to self-hatred and the belief that Whites are superior to African Americans ?

Environment

Many central city African-Americans are living in communities that are run-down. In these communities, the parks have not been cleaned in years, sidewalks have not been fixed and schools appear to be falling apart. I had a client who lived in a lower-class African-American community who informed me that the local elementary school did not have enough books and seats for the students. She went on to state that her children are very aware that they are poor. A run-down environment can have a negative impact on ones self-concept, for you are very aware of the fact that others are living under better conditions.

Self-Hate As A Contributing Factor To Addiction

When people hate themselves, they will do bad things to themselves. It is just that simple! One popular method of self-destruction is addiction. Many African-Americans today are medicating their self-contempt and self-hate with chemicals. If you are under the anesthetic influence of chemicals, you won't have to feel the pain of self-loathing. The "Self-Hate Model" is a major causal factor in the development of addiction in African-Americans. I have traveled throughout the United States and seen entire African-American communities that have been wiped-out by addiction. Perhaps we should begin to view this problem as being more profound than individual addiction. Perhaps in such communities what we are really seeing is community self-hate being medicated by chemicals. The implication is that the solution should also be community based. Nancy Reagan's strategy of "Just Say No" was an ineffective force because if I hate myself and "say no" to drugs, I will say yes to some other self-destructive behavior. Any prevention program that is serious about dealing with substance abuse and young African American males will deal with the issue of self hate.

African-American Males And Self-Hate

In my private practice, I work with a number of African-American males who have five to ten years of sobriety. What I have learned in working with these men is that self-hate often lies underneath the addiction. It has been my experience that people are ready to deal with issues of self-hate more intensely, after they have been sober for a significant period of time. It is often too painful for many recovering individuals to take a good look at themselves early in recovery. As these men begin to deal with issues of self-hate, they automatically become more self-actualized. As this natural momentum continues, they begin to want to do more for their family, community, race and the world (in that order).

This would not be possible without a strong recovery foundation. Adults are better equipped to eventually deal with issues of self-hate after they have had some quality sobriety. This is why it is imperative for detox, inpatient, day treatment, outpatient and intensive outpatient programs to do a better job of helping people with early stage recovery. This involves providing more individualized treatment and the recognition of the fact that clients bring their cultural issues with them into the treatment milieu.

CHAPTER III

THE DISPROPORTIONATE REPRESENTATION OF AFRICAN AMERICAN MALES IN TREATMENT

African American males, as a collective group, have several characteristics in common with Adult Children of Alcoholics. Just as the ACOA is more vulnerable to developing an addiction than the general population, so is the African American male.

According to Claudia Black, in the book "It will never

happen to me", Children of alcoholic parents often grow up living with three unwritten, rigid rules. These rules are "Don't talk, Don't trust, Don't feel". As a result, the child grows up with a huge void and will often turn to mood altering chemicals to fill that void.

The environment has also led many African American men to abide by these same three rules. In our society, if they talk about their experiences, they are looked upon as being a militant, radical, racist, communist or un-American. Thus, many African American men will abide by the "don't talk" rule to avoid negative labels and negative attention. This experience is quite similar to the young COA who breaks the "Don't talk" rule in their alcoholic family. They are often ostracized and scapegoated by their family.

Many African American men also operate under the "Don't trust" rule. Discrimination, racism and exploitation have led to their adherence to the "don't trust" rule. They also develop a lack of trust when dealing with other African Americans because, more often than not, if they are a victim of a petty crime, their perpetrator is often another African-American male.

They operate under the "Don't Feel" rule because society has conditioned them to believe that they are supposed to be a super-masculine man. Super-masculine men do not share feelings. This is reinforced as young African American boys are labeled as "weak" by their peers if they share feelings. Throughout their history in America, African American males have had to endure a great deal of pain and suffering. Like children of alcoholics it is common for African American males to deny or bury their feelings related to these experiences. This is the same protective defense used by children of alcoholics to avoid feeling the pain of growing up in an alcoholic home. Even the African American male who has been labeled an "Uncle Tom" often buried their feelings related to the racism and discrimination that they have experienced, because the feelings might be to painful. They are like the COA who has experienced trauma, such as physical and/or sexual abuse. Some African Americans are able to block painful experiences related to being African

American from their conscious awareness.

African American males operating under these three rules, like the COA, may drink alcohol, smoke marijuana and experiment with other drugs, etc. for the same reasons that others do. However, they may soon learn that these drugs medicate their condition and this may quickly lead to addiction. Thus, like adult children of alcoholics, African American males are disproportionately well-represented in substance abuse treatment.

In addition to the three rules previously mentioned, the African American male also has other characteristics in common with ACOA's. Below are some common characteristics of adult children of alcoholics with explanations of how they relate to the experience of the African American male and of how they play a role in substance abuse:

Characteristic: ACOA's Feel Guilty When They Stand Up For Themselves.

Many African Americans have a long history of not assert-ing themselves in situations in which they feel exploited. Thus, when an effort is made for them to assert themselves they feel uncomfortable and guilty. They feel guilty be-cause, like children of alcoholics, their condition has af-fected their self-esteem and they blame themselves for their circumstance. The African American male may soon learn that by getting drunk they are able to be more assertive. Unfortunately, this often ends in an arrest for disorderly conduct. They soon learn that marijuana can give them the confidence to stand up for themselves or that heroin will numb them from the powerlessness that they feel. Every time they feel guilty for using heroin, they can use more heroin to block out the reality of those painful feelings.

Characteristic: Many ACOA's Have Stuffed Their Feel-ings From Their Traumatic Childhoods And Have Lost The Ability To Feel Or Express Feelings Because It Hurts So Much.

The African American male learns that drugs have the ability to kill the pain of negative feelings caused by environmental stress. It has been documented that certain strains of mice prefer water to alcohol. When an electric shock is administered to a caged mouse, they will learn by trial and error that by drinking the alcohol, they can stop the electric shock. Later, as time progressed these same mice preferred the alcohol over the water. These mice medicated themselves to avoid the harshness of their environment and as a result, developed an addiction to alcohol. It is believed that some African-American males may do the same thing. Harboring feelings of low self-esteem, dealing with traumatic feelings related to a painful childhood and frustrated for not reaching the "American Dream", they may medicate their condition with alcohol, cocaine, heroin, marijuana, etc.

Characteristic: ACOA's Tend To Look For Immediate Rather Than Deferred Gratification.

African American leaders throughout history have always felt the need to bring the message of hope (future-related hope) to African American followers. These leaders recognize that many African Americans lack hope for the future and they tend to look for immediate rather than deferred gratification. The poverty experience taught many African Americans to take care of immediate needs.

Drug abuse is perfect for this kind of orientation because it offers an immediate gratification. This becomes a relapse issue for the recovering African American male who, like the ACOA, has difficulty delaying gratification and often does not have much practice completing activities that have delayed rewards.

I am terming the condition that increases the probability that an African American male will become chemically dependent "The African American Male Environmental Syndrome" which has much in common with the Adult Children Of Alcoholics Syndrome. Other characteristics that African American males have in common with ACOA's are listed below:

1. They live from the viewpoint of victims.
2. They are addicted to excitement.

3. They judge themselves harshly.
4. They are reactors rather than actors.
5. They guess at what's normal.
6. They fear authority figures and personal criticism.
7. They have difficulty following a project through from beginning to end.
8. They usually feel different from other people.
9. They generally over-react out of fear.

Like the ACOA, all of these characteristics may not apply to every African American male, but many are very commonly observed. The African American male may not be the only group that has similar characteristics to ACOA's. Citizens of the former Soviet Union tend to drink vodka abundantly, perhaps as a result of having lived in a communist society that operated like an alcoholic family. Just like an untreated alcoholic family, the system in Russia was a closed system, that operated under the "Don't talk, Don't trust, Don't feel" rules. Masses of people were controlled by a few individuals in the same way that an actively drinking alcoholic is able to control their family system. The Native Americans may be another classic example of a people operating under the same three rules and thus they have tended to medicate their condition with alcohol.

I am very aware of the latest research that suggests that there is a genetic predisposition to alcoholism and I agree with this research. I also believe that genetics alone does not come close to explaining the disproportionate representation of African American males in treatment.

CHAPTER IV

FEELINGS, AND THE AFRICAN-AMERICAN MALE SUBSTANCE ABUSER

I have spent a year observing a trained professional do psychodrama groups with a substance abusers on an inpatient unit. Following the emotional drama, patients had the opportunity to discuss their feelings related to the experience. Week after week, I observed that African-American males had the toughest time sharing feelings in the group. Following the group activities the staff members would meet and were usually always perplexed about how to get the African-American male clients to express their feelings. This difficulty in talking about feelings is not a new phenomenon for the African-American male.

Historically, there were certain African societies in which it was not considered masculine to show fears and anxiety, in fact showing fears was considered to be feminine. African-American males are the descendants of this tradition prior to slavery. During slavery, African-American males endured a great deal of suffering. The psychological response was to turn off their feelings to deny them.

Following slavery many African American males moved North and lived in poverty. While living in the North, many African American males felt the need to appear to be tough to hide fears. This was often a defense against real and/or imagined danger. Remember, in poor neighborhoods with a violent, high crime rate, gang-related behavior flourishes. Acting tough, hiding vulnerabilities and fears is a way to avoid being victimized by crime and gang-related behavior.

My grandfather told me a story about his experience while riding a donkey. He told me that if the donkey felt that you were afraid, he would kick you. In order to avoid being kicked by the donkey you would have to turn off your feelings and pretend that you were not afraid. Many African-American males have developed a similar ability. Particularly central city youth who learn to hide their fears to avoid being attacked by others.

One emotion that may appear to dominate African-American male substance abusers is anger. Often unable to express feelings openly, they will allow anger to build until they explode. Many counselors will refuse to confront them on treatment issues because they are afraid they will get angry. As clinicians we must get rid of our unrealistic fears of the African-American male's anger. We should examine our deep-seated fears about their anger and then test it with reality. Being less afraid of African-American males should make it easier to confront them. At times they may use their anger as a defense. Many African-American males have learned that they can get others to avoid confronting them by pretending to be angry.

Regardless of their past, as clients they will need to be supported more than confronted. We will be unsuccessful as therapists fighting fire with fire. Although we may assume that they are angry, the underlying feeling is often fear. Fear of being discovered, of vulnerability or of what will happen if they share their feelings.

Clinicians often become frustrated because of the difficulty involved in getting African American males to express their feelings. This frustration often leads to a clinical explanation on the part of the therapist. Unfortunately this explanation often includes a diagnosis of personality disorder. (Often the anti-social personality disorder). Since I have been working in the chemical dependence field I have seen more African American males receive a diagnosis of anti-social personality than any other treatment population. The labeling could have a negative impact upon how we view African American males because the prognosis for clients suffering from personality disorders is poor.

I have presented historical data with the hope of increasing our empathetic understanding of the reasons it might be difficult for this population to share feelings. I do not pretend to have the solution. I hope that we will continue to examine this issue. For now, I offer the following suggestions to the therapist:

1. Be patient. Recognize that the African American male's history plays a key role in their difficulty in sharing feelings. We will not be able to force them to share feelings. They may perceive the forceful effort as a threat.

2. If they are unable to identify a feeling, give them two or three options, but do not identify the feeling for them.

3. Do not be afraid of their anger. As stated earlier, their anger is often a defense. More times than not, they will respect you if you confront their anger.

4. Prepare for the possibility that African-American males may cry. It is important for clinicians not to give verbal or nonverbal messages indicating that they should not cry. Often, as a child they were told that "men don't cry".

5. Talk about your own feelings with the African-

American male. This makes it easier for them to share feelings with you.

CHAPTER V

The African American Male Spirituality, Religion and Powerlessness

AA's First Step:

> We admitted we were powerless over alcohol and that
> our life has become unmanageable.

Aesop tells a fable about a little gnat that defeated a lion in battle. While flying away feeling proud and victorious, he was tangled in a spider's web. Prior to being devoured by the spider the gnat said his final words. In essence, he pointed out how difficult it is to admit to being powerless over the smallest of creatures (the spider) after defeating the most powerful (the lion).

The African-American male may have a similar struggle admitting powerlessness over a glass of beer, a small pill, white powder, a single marijuana cigarette, etc., after being conditioned by society to believe that they are strong and powerful. This is not a reference to financial or economic power. They have been conditioned to believe that they are physically strong, cannot be overtaken by emotions and can handle anything. This conditioning can be detrimental to their sobriety, for AA's First Step states that an alcoholic must admit that they are powerless. Clinicians must recognize that the notion of powerlessness will be foreign to many African-American males.

Another problem faced by African-American men is the notion of spirituality versus religion. One big complaint in the African-American community is that the church is mostly filled with women and children. The African-American man has often dropped out of the church, fed up with the organized religion and the belief that the church can help them with their problems. It appears that many have also given up on the belief that God will help them with their problems.

As African American males are introduced to 12 step groups many hear the term "spiritual program", and think religion. We must work hard to explain the difference between religion and spirituality. Some African American males may blame God for their plight. Although they do not hold the monopoly on this issue, many African American males are angry with God. Regardless of your religious orientation, allow them to express their angry feelings toward God. God is big enough and can handle their feelings and complaints. They may believe that God has not been available to them in all the years that they have been suffering. They may even utilize this as an excuse to get high. We must confront the African-American male about the possibility that their addiction may have contributed to their problems. The client may say, "Yeah, but what about racism and discrimination?" Reality therapy, would be very effective in such a case. Clinicians cannot change racism from the "clinical" chair. At the same time we should not ignore the fact that racism exists in our society. Clients must be presented with the reality of what they can and cannot change. They will respect the therapist for being honest. The greatest hope is that once the African-American male clears their mind, body and soul of mood-altering chemicals they will be in a better position to fight injustices.

It is also my belief that a percentage of African-American males were religiously abused as children, in that their parents used extremely strict religious rules to protect their children from the outside environment. These rules included "God does not want you to play, God does not want you to watch TV, God does not want you to listen to popular music or God is going to get you".

Many African American males in treatment still believe that

"God is going to get me". It may take time for some African American males to develop a notion of a "loving God", as referred to in the 12-Step literature of AA.

Clinicians should also recognize that while they are teaching the disease concept of addiction in treatment, many African American male clients are still thinking "sin concept". The African American church for years has preached "sin concept". I recommend that treatment facilities begin taking thorough religious histories in an effort to determine if clients have been religiously abused and if the client is unable to grasp the disease concept because of the belief in the "sin concept".

CHAPTER VI

The African American Male and Other Addictions

Gambling

Many addicts are vulnerable to developing other addictions following abstinence from drugs. These addictions include eating disorders, sexual addictions, gambling, compulsive spending, etc. It is believed that the African-American male is often vulnerable to a gambling problem before, during and after their active drug abuse.

Sociologists have pointed out that the poor and the wealthy use the notion of "luck" to explain their position in life. If you ask the rich the reason for their success they may respond by stating that they have "good luck". They will say this to avoid sounding as if they are bragging or to avoid giving the impression that they possess special power. If you ask the poor the reason for their position in life they will often respond by saying that they have "bad luck".

Many African-American males believe that they have bad luck. On an unconscious level they begin to think that life is controlled by "luck" rather than by a higher power. Thus, they are very vulnerable to excessive gambling.

Statistics show that the lottery is played in the African-American community in disproportionately high numbers. In Chicago, the lottery lines are much longer in African-American communities than they are in other ethnic communities. In Harlem, in addition to the state lottery, there are numerous underground lotteries operating continuously.

Besides the lottery, there are other forms of gambling that are popular among African-American males; dice, spades, bid whisk, gin-rummy, poker, pool, etc.; although many of these games of chance may not be popular in Las Vegas or Atlantic City, they should be taken serious by clinicians. Problems with these forms of gambling can still meet the DSM-III-R classification for compulsive gambling.

Another reason that this issue is important is because it is extremely difficult to worship "luck" and believe in a higher power at the same time. Clinicians treating African-American male substance abusers should be aware of how a strong belief in "luck" can affect their ability to conceptualize and believe in a "power greater than self".

Eating Disorders

Traditionally on holidays such as Christmas, Independence Day, New Years, Thanksgiving, etc., African Americans have been known to eat large feasts. In many African American families, children are encouraged to eat every drop of food on their plate. Some are told by their parents

"Child, you better eat every drop of that food on your plate, don't you know that there are children in Africa who are starving. Who are you to throw away food?"

Such an attitude about food can produce the tendency to overeat. Eating is also a way of helping those who feel deprived, feel full and less deprived. African-American men who are ACOA's or who are from other types of dysfunctional families are very vulnerable to becoming compulsive overeaters. These children often feel unloved and therefore, they turn to substances such as drugs and food to help fill the void. The African-American "soul food" diet of fats, sugar and starch is highly addictive.

Usually if a compulsive overeater develops an addiction to alcohol or other drugs, they will more than likely stop eating compulsively because the drug becomes their "food". The tendency to eat compulsively will probably become an issue again when they become abstinent from drugs. Eating can help them avoid the abundance of feelings that emerge when drug use is stopped.

It is appropriate for clinicians to do assessments for compulsive overeating, for it can definitely have relapse implications. Bulimia and anorexia do not seem to occur as often with African-Americans as it does within other ethnic groups.

In the book "beyond Therapy, Beyond Science", Ann Wilson Schaef mentioned that rarely does an addict have just one addiction. The African-American male substance abuser is no exception. He is vulnerable to the wide range of other addictions. More gamblers Anonymous, over enters anonymous, debters anonymous and other 12 step groups are needed in African American communities.

CHAPTER VII

Sex And The African-American Male Substance Abuser

The myth of the African American male's sexual superiority can have a negative impact on those African American males in need of substance abuse treatment. This is one myth that has been around for so long that it is accepted by many as fact. Thus, when alcohol, cocaine, speed, etc., begin to affect their ability to achieve and maintain an erection, this may cause major stress for the African-American male, especially if they have accepted this societal myth. It will cause even more stress if their sexual partner has also accepted the myth of African American male sexual superiority and the performance criteria that accompanies it.

The African-American males may feel extremely sensitive about this subject, yet they may keep all their feelings about this issue to themselves. The counselor may need to bring this subject up, because secrecy, shame, embarrassment and silence can lead to relapse. Clinicians should learn to feel comfortable in asking the African-American male sexual questions. This subject can also be discussed in lectures. The African-American man's feelings need to be normalized. We must start the process of dispelling the myth of African American male sexual superiority with factual information.

Some African American males in treatment will point out that their original attraction to cocaine was when they were told that the drug increases sexual potency. Cocaine's depletion of dopamine in the brain in fact leads to decreased sexual drive and potency. Many African American males deal with this anxiety by getting together with other African American men on treatment units and bragging about "incredible" sexual accomplishments. They also need an avenue to talk about sexual performance fears. One method of dealing with this aspect of treatment is to hire a sex therapist who can do group educational lectures and meet with clients individually to discuss sexual concerns.

CHAPTER VIII

The African-American Male Substance Abuser Who Sells Drugs

Dealers are entrepreneurs. It is not uncommon in some African-American communities for children to admire drug dealers. Before the addiction takes over, the dealer is able to buy numerous material items. The dealer is also in the spotlight as customers approach them for their product. They may carry a beeper, which is a social status symbol.

For the African-American male being a dealer can mean not having to climb up the corporate ladder, avoiding memos, verbal and written warnings, arbitration, suspensions, racism and subtle forms of discrimination in hiring. It means beating the odds. Only a small percentage of African-Americans are entrepreneurs. It will be hard for them to give up dealing because it offers them a certain freedom. While in treatment, they often think that they can stop using the drug and continue selling it. We know that this almost always leads to a return to substance use.

The African American male substance abuser/dealer does not always sell the drug for selfish reasons. Many begin selling drugs part-time to supplement a low income.

I know of African American men who have initially used this extra income for rent, child support payments, to help keep their family off welfare, etc. Obviously, as the addiction progresses, they use the money primarily to feed the addiction. Recognizing that some of the money has been put to good use, they may rationalize that it is okay to continue selling drugs.

The clinician who says to the African American male client "you have to give up selling drugs" will probably not be effective. The therapist should examine what "dealing" means to the individual, what they get out of it, the pros versus the cons and what life would be like for them without selling the drugs.

CHAPTER IX

Family Relationships, Friendships, Associates And The African-American Male Substance Abuser

African American men traditionally have a strong connection with their mother. When elementary age African American male children are signifying (talking negative about each other), the worst thing that one could say about the other is something negative about that person's mother. This often ends in a fight. When adult African American male colleague or professional athletes are given the chance to talk on national television following a victory, the first words they utter are "Hi, Mom".

While this bond is special, the relationship between the African American mother and her adult son can be enmeshed and become a real issue in treatment. When they get into trouble as a result of addiction and can't run to anyone else, their mothers often rescue them, thus serving as a primary enabler. Part of family therapy should be geared towards untangling this often enmeshed bond, allowing the client the space and opportunity to grow. Clinicians need to proceed slowly in intervening in this dyad. It often works best if the clinician establishes a trusting relationship with the clients' mother before trying to change the system. She will often perceive the abruptness of the intervention as a threat. If the mother is enabling, it is out of love, therefore very patient and caring intervetions are needed.

The relationship between the African American male substance abuser and their father is often filled with love and anger. Their father is often upset with them because of the negative behavior caused by the addiction. The anger often effects the father's ability to express the love.

The family may try to keep dad out of the family therapy process because of his discomfort. The therapist should work hard to involve him in the therapeutic process because he is an important part of the family system.

RELATIONSHIPS

There are four types of intimate relationships that are very common among African-American male substance abusers:

Type 1

A relatively healthy relationship despite the fact that the woman is codependent and the male is addicted. If both are motivated to work recovery programs, this type of relationship often turns out fine.

Type 2

A relationship in which the male is totally dominant. This type of relationship is often observed in treatment and is very understandable. When men feel they are not in control of their destiny, because of lack of opportunity, racism, discrimination, etc.,, they feel they must control something. The target is often the person with whom they are in an intimate relationship. This presents special problems in treatment. For one thing, the African American male may not want their partner to be involve in their treatment for fear of losing control of her. Therapists must work hard to allow them to talk about this ambivalence and their fear related to losing control. Since the woman may not be use to asserting herself, the therapist may need to make a special effort to reach out in order to involve her in treatment. Part of the therapeutic goal should be geared towards empowering the spouse through the use of therapeutic spouse groups and/or self-help groups which would help take her out of the role of an enabler.

Type 3

A relationship in which the chemically dependent male is dominated by the spouse. Often the spouse is a carbon copy of their mother and their relationship could be similar to the relationship they observed between their parents; an over-adequate/under-adequate relationship. She often functions as a primary enabler and her feeling of self-worth and importance are enhanced as she takes care of the addict. She is often an ACOA, her father usually being the addicted parent. Since she dominates the relationship, the addict is able to use the relationship as an excuse to continue getting high. "I'm a victim, therefore I have a right to get high". "She nags too much, tells me what to do all the time, so I must get high in order to deal with her". Therapy in this situation involves helping them see their role in the addiction. Helping the addict see that they use the relationship as an excuse to get high is essential. Furthermore, the therapist must help her get in touch with unresolved ACOA issues, especially the need to control. The woman should be encouraged to work an ACOA or Alanon program. Systemic couples therapy could be instrumental in helping to change the relationship from an over-adequate/under-adequate relationship to one of more equality.

Type 4

A relationship in which they are both chemically dependent. Statistically, the chances of both members remaining sober are not very great. When one starts the process of relapse, the other often starts to go in the same direction. They should be encouraged to work their own separate recovery programs. Recommendations for separate post-treatment halfway house placements should be made for this type of couple. Such placement for both parties is recommended because a great deal of jealousy exists within these couples. They will rarely accept a recommendation for one of them to go into a halfway house without the partner going too. They fear that they will lose their partner while in the halfway house setting.

Friendships and Associates

When assessing who the African American male spends

their leisure time with, clinicians need to differentiate be-tween friends and "associates".

African American males will call most of the people they meet during the active stages of their addiction "associates". They include drug-dealers and people with whom they get high.

They usually consider their "friends" to be people that they grew up with prior to the addiction. Some of these friends may date back to elementary and high school. There might be a few individuals in the "old friends" category with whom the client currently gets high.

Counselors should encourage the client to avoid "associates" and to establish new or rekindle old friendships. Caution should be taken when talking to clients about their future interactions with "old friends" with whom they currently get high with. The thing that makes this relationship unique is that clients often had clean fun with these individuals before their drug use. These are often the most difficult relationships to give up. The counselor should give the client room to talk about the entire relationship. The "good old days" and their recent drug use should be addressed together. The client should also be encouraged to talk about ambivalent feelings related to the relationship. The negative and positive aspects of remaining in the relationship should be explored.

CHAPTER X

White Counselors Working With African-American Male Substance Abusers

The greater the level of empathy, the more effective the white counselor will be working with African-American male substance abusers. There are three levels of empathy:

<u>Level One Empathy</u>

<u>Understanding About a person</u>. This level of empathy is the

least effective. It involves understanding another person based upon what you see on TV, read in the papers or hear through gossip. Those using this method as their primary way of understanding the African American male will probably be ineffective as a helper. Far too often, TV portrays African American males in stereotypical negative roles, such as pimps, hustlers, thieves, swindlers, etc. They are almost always portrayed as being extremely angry. The media frequently portrays African American males in a less than admirable light. White counselors whose primary form of empathy is level one empathy will be ineffective with African American males.

Level Two Empathy

Understanding another through our own experiences. This is mostly a mental exercise in which the counselor imagines what it would be like to be a African American male. They think about some of the issues that confront and shape the world view of African American men, such as institutional racism, victimization, religion, the family, etc. Then the counselor thinks about similarities that they have experienced in their own lives. While trying to understand the world view of the African American male, the White female counselor can become empathetic by getting in touch with her feelings related to being female in male-dominated society.

Level Three Empathy

Understanding the experiences of the client. This is the highest level of empathy. It involves the process of under-standing the African American male individually, through their own unique individual experiences. This level of empathy requires the counselor to make a special effort to avoid lumping all African American males into one category.

The counselor practicing Level 3 empathy should ask them-selves a series of questions about each African American male client. These questions include:

1. How would I feel if I were this individual?

2. How do they view sobriety?

3. What has been their experience with racism?

4. How do they feel about whites?

5. How do they feel about having a White counselor?

6. What would it be like to be them?

7. How is their experience different than mine?

8. How is their experience similar to mine?

9. What is their internal world like?

Answers to these questions may become clearer as the clinician strives to build a relationship with the client. Having a sensitive discussion about race (i.e., asking African American male clients about their feelings about working with a White counselor) can often be instrumental in opening up the lines of communication.

Sympathy

When working with African-American males, it is important to adopt an empathetic rather than a sympathetic stance. Counselors who feel sorry for their clients are easy to manipulate. The white counselor who has the tendency to feel sorry for the African American male client because they have experienced racism and discrimination should remember that the same racism produced Dr. Martin Luther King, Jr., George Washington Carver, Frederick Douglas, etc. The counselor may say the individual's just mentioned are the exception rather than the rule. This is true. It is also important to remember that they did not make strides because people were feeling sorry for them.

Guilt

Guilt about injustices done to African-Americans by white society often gets in the way of white counselors delivering effective services to African American male clients. Each counselor is only responsible for their own behavior. If the counselor is not involved in exploiting African Americans, in any way, there is no reason to feel guilty. This guilt can often keep the white counselor from confronting African American clients and from having sensitive discussions with African American clients about issues such as race. Some African American clients will unconsciously push the "guilt button" of their white counselor as a defense against being confronted in treatment. It is guilt that stops a white counselor from asking a African American male client if they think racism or discrimination is involved when the client gives subtle hints about their poor relationship with a supervisor at work, difficulty in getting a bank loan, feeling that they had to wait too long to be served in a restaurant, etc.

Fear

One of the greatest barriers for white counselors working with African-American male substance abusers is fear. Yet again, the media plays a big part in helping to spark this fear, by focusing a great deal of attention on African American males committing crime. Following the 1992 riots in Los Angeles, I saw a commercial on T.V. that advertised self-defense classes. The commercial switched back and forth between two scenes. One scene showed white students taking the self-defense class and the other scene showed African Americans beating up on whites during the L.A. riots. The message is, whites need to defend themselves against African Americans . This type of media advertisement increases the tensions between the races.

Many white women have a pronounced fear of African-American males. There are probably few African-American males who have not had the experience of walking down the street past a white female and her clutching her purse as if he were a purse-snatcher. What is the origin of this fear? Oral tradition in the African American community suggest that during slavery, white males had sexual desires for African American women so they wanted to make sure that there would be no sexual relations between white women and African American men. They placed white women on pedestals and discouraged any contact between white women and African American men. Another method that was use was to try to convince white women that African American men were rapists. The media continues to perpetrate this fear. Most white women who are raped, are raped by white men, usually someone they know. Most African American women who are raped, are raped by African American men, usually someone they know also. Are white female counselors immune to the before-mentioned fears? How does being fearful affect the therapeutic relationship as they work with African American males?

Tension Between White And African American Males

There has been a tension in America between White and African American males since slavery. How often is this tension openly talked about? Why hasn't a peace treaty or an open forum been called to discuss this historic male to male tension? Both sides generally deal with the tension by avoiding each other. Often when African American and White males occupy the same space socially, they need a triangulator (alcohol) to ease the tension. How does this tension between African American and white males in America effect the cross-cultural counseling relationship? How often is the tension acknowledged in counseling?

A Lesson From The South

Recently, when ever there are reports of riots and major racial conflicts, the reports come from the East coast, west coast or the midwest region. Rarely, are there any reports about major racial conflict in the southern states.

The south used to be the capital of race riots. How has this change occurred? Let's go back into history for the answer. Following the Civil War, Northern politicians placed former African American slaves in leadership positions over their former slave masters. This maneuver lessened the tension between whites in the North and South, but increased the tension between African Americans and Whites in the south. The KKK emerged as a means of violently dealing with this shift in power. African Americans and Whites in the south have been open about their dislike of and mistrust of each other since the Reconstruction Era. There are fewer racial outbursts in the south today because African Americans and Whites in the South have for long periods of time had open discussions about their true feelings for each other. White counselors working with African American males could learn from this lesson.

How To Have A Sensitive Discussion About Race

It is my belief that it is most effective to discuss the issue of race in therapy when it becomes a concern of the clients. Most African American clients will not come out directly and talk to their white counselor about discomfort in working with them. They will often bring the subject up by talking about injustices that the experienced in society or their experiences with whites in society. This is an opportunity for the therapist to ask the client what it is like for him to be working with a white therapist. It is often useful to have a sensitive discussion about race in the early stages of the therapeutic relationship. It is also sometimes helpful to talk about issues of race in the middle and later stage of the therapeutic ralationship, if race becomes an issue in those stages. Clinicians will need to listen with "a third ear" for possible evidence that race is effecting the therapeutic relationship and be willing to talk about it. Clinicians also need to be consciously aware of their own biases so that they will not blindly or unconsciously damage the relationship.

The following are excerpts from two counseling interviews. The first interview with a recovering African-American male substance abuser discussing his experience of working with white counselors. The second interview is with a white female counselor, who describes her experience of working with African-American male substance abusers.

Interview #1

The following interview was conducted with Mike, who has been sober for 9 years.

Interviewer: "Mike, tell me about your addiction".

Mike: "My addiction started when I was a teenager. I have used all kinds of drugs, my drug of choice is heroin. My addiction has led me in and out of jail for a majority of my life".

Interviewer: "Did you have both African American and White counselors when you were in treatment?"

Mike: "I was in a court-ordered residential treatment facility for two years. I have been sober ever since. I had two counselors and they were both white".

Interviewer: "Tell me about your experience with those two counselors".

Mike: "I worked with one counselor for the first 15 months I was in treatment. He was a recovering addict, but I still didn't feel close to him because our worlds were so different. He did what I called 'generic counseling'. All he would do was focus on my addiction. Hell, I was from the ghetto. The ghetto had as much of a hold on me as my addiction. I would leave treatment and go to my old neighbor hood and spend time with people I used to get high with. He would never address my going home. He was not interested in my world and lacked cultural-sensitivity. It was more like a police/offender relationship".

Interviewer: "Did the two of you ever have open discus sions about race?"

Mike: "No. Sometimes, I think he would sense my discomfort and he would try to prove to me that he had African American friends. To tell you the truth, it was my peers and the brief contact that I had with a few African Ameri can counselors that helped me stay sober for those first 15 months".

Interviewer: "What would have made this a better rela tionship?"

Mike: "My counselor could have explored how I felt about him. He could have been interested enough in me to want to know about my world. I felt that he was a white guy who was not interested in African Americans".

Interviewer: "What about your experience with the second counselor?"

Mike: "My second counselor was also White. We had a good relationship because he was more down to earth. He was an immigrant from Czechoslovakia. As soon as we began work ing together, he shared his childhood experi ence with racism, being a poor immigrant and living in America. He went on to share with me that he began to sell drugs at a very early age to help support his family and then wound up in Cook County jail. He told me that while he was in jail, some African American in mates stole his shoes. As a result of that experience he began to see all African Ameri cans as being intimidators, non-trust worthy and thugs. He had to gradually learn to trust African Americans again. Having this posi- tive experience with this white counselor helped me clear up my prejudice with the whole white race. I learned to individualize my interactions with people."

Interviewer: "Tell me about other interactions with the second counselor."

Mike: "He had a sense of humor. He was willing to join my world, validate my feelings and he was interested in more than just my addic tion. He would take all my negative street characteristics and turn them into positive attributes."

EXERCISE #1

In the space below, answer the following questions:

1. Why did Mike's relationship with his first counselor fail?

2.　If you were the counselor, how would you have worked with Mike?

3.　What did the second counselor do to help build a positive working relationship with Mike?

The second interview is with June, a licensed clinical social worker and certified addictions counselor.

Interviewer:　"Tell me about your experience counseling African-American male substance abusers."

June:　"Most of my experience was on an inpatient substance abuse unit. I believe that I was quite effective in working with this special population."

Interviewer: "What made you effective?"

June: " I would have open discussions with them
               about race. During individual sessions, I
               would also talk to them about their anger.
               Many of these men witnessed a great deal of
               violence while growing up. Experiencing
               racism, along with deprivation made them
               very angry. I would let them know that I was
               not afraid of their anger. During group ses
               sions, I would challenge them on specific
               issues. I was consciously aware that African
               American clients often view white workers
               as lazy,because they don't challenge them or
               confront them on issues. Knowing that, they
               don't confront or challenge them out of fear,
               I did not want to be perceived as being lazy."

THE JOY OF CROSS-CULTURAL COUNSELING

I have personally had the opportunity to work with individuals from all over the world. This experience has giving me
a much greater connection with the human race. I find
people very interesting! This cross-cultural work has opened
up my eyes to what is gong on in the world. These clients
have been my "windows" to the world. I am able to travel
mentally by listening to their world experiences. Working
with one population would not be nearly as educational,

exciting, or challenging. One of the things that has contributed to my success in cross-cultural counseling is that I allow my clients to be teachers of their culture. I take a curious, rather than "all knowing" posture.

Many counselors approach cross cultural counseling as if they are the authority on the clients culture. Others ignore cultural issues completely, while others try to change the clients cultural beliefs. These methods build therapeutic walls rather than bridges and the counselor often blames the victim (the client), when no rapport is developed. Some counselors deal with this frustration by only working with clients whose backgrounds are just like theirs. These counselors will never really have the opportunity to experience the positive joy of cross cultural counseling.

CHAPTER XI

African American Counselors Working With African American Male Substance Abusers

All other things being equal, the African American counselor has a slight advantage in the area of working with African American male substance abusers. The African American counselor has also had an "African American experience". However, the African American counselor will still need to work hard to understand the client through the client's unique experiences. It is important not to lump all African American male clients in the same cultural category. I met an African American male who was born and reared in Japan. Does he have the same cultural experience as African American males reared on the west side of Chicago? I have worked with the African American clients who grew up in predominately white neighborhood, who were extremely uncomfortable receiving treatment in predominately African American treatment facilities.

Class differences between the African American client and counselor can also be a barrier in treatment. It is important to be able to talk about these differences and to allow the client to be the teacher about their cultural experience.

African American males have often been socialized to avoid expressing feelings and having to always appear to be "strong". Especially in the presence of another African American male. The African American male counselor/ client relationship offers the opportunity for the African American male client to learn to express feelings and vulnerabilities in the presence of another African American male. It is important that the counselor not send verbal or non verbal messages that it is not ok for the client to express their feelings, or show vulnerabilities. They even need to know that it is ok to cry.

African American female counselors have talked openly about their difficulty in counseling African American male clients. The African American male client may have the desire to treat their African American female counselor the same way that they treat other females in their life. If she is older, they may want to treat her the way they treat their mother or grandmother. If they are approximately the same age, which is usually the case they may want to treat her the way they treat their girlfriend or wife. Being called "honey", "dear", "baby" and darling by African American male clients often stirs up strong negative countertransference feelings for the African American female counselor. This is often very frustrating for the African American female counselor because she wants to be viewed as a therapeutic change agent by the African American male, not as a potential girlfriend. She will need to be patient, persistent and consistent in these situations. Good clinical skills will allow her to work through this identification crisis. It is important to realize that the current tension that exists in America between African American men and women can also be present in the therapeutic relationship. As these issues arise they can be disccussed as a part of treatment.

On Dealing With The Issue Of Racism

There needs to be a balance between the client talking about the racism they have experienced and working on recovery.

Often when the chemically dependent client continuously talks about racism in therapy, it is the workers needs that are being met by this dialogue. Given the fact that African American counselors also experience racism in their lives, it can be tempting to allow the client to go off on tangents on this subject.

It is important for the counselor not to over identify with this experience. It is equally important for the counselor not to deny the client's reality. Over identification can sometimes make it difficult for the counselor to remain objective and the client may begin to counsel the counselor.

An additional reason to avoid identifying too strongly is that from our therapeutic chair we cannot change society. The main thing the substance abuse counselor can do is to help the client change their behavior and response to society. Counselors who participate with the client in blaming society for all the client's problems can indirectly help the client feel like a victim, thus giving them a rationalization for continuing to abuse drugs.

Following are excerpts from an interview with a African American male and female counselor describing their experience of working with African-American male substance abusers.

Tim is a 42-year old African-American male who has been working in the addictions field for 9 years.

Interviewer: "Tell me about your experience treating African-American male substance abusers".

Tim: "Regardless of what the literature states, I think substance abuse in African American males has a lot to do with their rites of pas sages. One sees their friends getting high and they join their friends. I see racism as having a great impact on African American males. I am therefore comfortable having discussions about race. I usually do not stay on this subject for long, so they will not use it as an excuse to keep getting high. I have a lot of strengths that help me work with African American males. One of my biggest strengths is being an African American male in America. By being a African American male I can talk their language. They not only bring their addiction to treatment, they also bring their African American experience".

Interviewer: "You're middle class and you have worked with poor African-American males. Has that ever been an issue?"

Tim: "No, because I know my stuff. I do not present myself as being better than anyone. I believe my presentation comes across as be ing knowledgeable and street wise at the same time. I am able to take the Jellinek's disease concept and explain it in a way that my clients can understand. I explain it so that it fits their experience".

Susan has an MSW and has been working in the Addictions fields for 8 years.

Interviewer: "Describe your experience counseling Afri can-American males with substance abuse problems."

Susan: "It has been an intriguing learning experience because of the multitude of personalities I have worked with. My being an African American female has been particularly inter esting, because of how African American males respond to me as a African American woman and because of how it becomes a part of the work we're doing."

"I have observed a number of dynamics. In a desire to avoid the work some clients would flirt with me. Others were not used to inter acting with African American women in positions of authority, so some would try not to respect me as a human being."

Interviewer: "How would they do this?"

Susan: "By not talking to me or by being friendly and charming with white workers while ignoring me. Some of them treated me really good, and those were very positive experiences. I think the ones who were disrespectful usually had unresolved issues to work out with their mothers and I would wind up taking the brunt of their anger."

Interviewer: "How would this affect you?"

Susan: "I would have to work hard not get caught up in their anger. I would process my feelings in supervision. One of the things that I am aware of is that there is a battle going on in America between Black men and Black women, because society paints the picture that Black women "wear the pants" in the family. This creates friction and can also effect the therapeutic relationship between Black men and women. Talking about these issues in supervision really helped me under stand the dynamics operating. As I was able to express my anger and other feelings in supervision I was able to be present for the client without bringing my anger into the situation. I was able to work through these issues with most of my clients who were Black males."

CHAPTER XII

A Word About The Future

In conclusion, there is a current trend towards outpatient rather than inpatient treatment. Increasingly, corporate America believes that in-patient treatment is too expensive and ineffective. I believe that history will prove that sending all the clients to out-patient treatment will not be a magical solution to the substance abuse problem and that a certain percentage of the population can benefit from in-patient treatment. A primary problem with in-patient treatment thus far is that it has not been sufficiently individualized. It has often resembled a factory assembly line, with everybody getting the exact same number of days and the same treatment.

More hospital-based treatment facilities are needed in poor African American communities for those who lack insurance to pay for treatment. The hospital environment offers a African American male the best opportunity to begin their sober journey for several reasons:

1. Being in a hospital offers the African American male an opportunity to temporarily leave the environment, which often plays a major role in the formation and continuation of their addiction. Hospital-based treatment also allows the addict to deal with issues in a safe environment, which would be very difficult to deal with outside, especially in the very earliest stages of recovery. These include: socializing with others without drugs, sharing feelings without drugs, dealing with authority (staff), interacting with peers, asserting him-

self, etc.

2. Many African American males are poly-drug users. This means that withdrawal is often a complicated matter. Hospital-based treatment allows them to focus on recovering while having on-going attention to their medical and detox needs.

3. The multidisciplinary team approach, which is often practiced in hospital settings, offers one of the most thorough methods of treating this physiological, psychological, environmental, emotional and spiritual illness.

More halfway houses and residential treatment facilities are needed to help the African American male with on-going recovery. More money will not have to be spent in building these facilities. This could be accomplished by reappropriating some of the money that is currently being used to deal with "The War On Drugs". Some of the money that is being utilized to build new prisons can be used to build substance abuse halfway houses. A justification for doing this exists, since such a high percentage of people in prison were under the influence of drugs while committing these crimes. The drug abuser who goes to jail without being treated for addiction, will more often than not, return to regular drug use when they are released from prison.

Throughout this book attention has been focused on the treatment needs of African-American male substance abusers. I encourage the reader to add to my list of observations, suggestions and recommendations.

ABOUT THE AUTHOR

Mark Sanders, LCSW, CADC

Mark Sanders has a Masters degree in Social Work from Loyola University of Chicago and is a Certified Addictions Counselor in the state of Illinois. His private practice in downtown Chicago specializes in the treatment of addiction, adult children of Alcoholics and Codependence.

A noted specialist in the substance abuse field. Mark is a

member of the faculty at Loyola University of Chicago School of Social Work. He is a consultant for numerous organizations on Substance abuse related issues.

Mark's experience in cross-cultural work is well established. He was the Program Director of the first southeast Asian and African Substance Abuse Counselor Training Program through the C.O.P.E. Training Institute in Chicago. He worked for a number of years as an international group facilitator for the Council on International Programs and presents seminars on cultural-diversity and cultural-specific treatment at the local and national level.